STARSDOWN

JASPER BERNES

Starsdown / Jasper Bernes . 2007

ingirumimusnocteetconsumimurigni

ISBN-13: 978-1-934639-02-3
ISBN-10: 1-934639-02-8

Distributed by Small Press Distribution (Berkeley, CA)
www.spdbooks.org

Book design by the author. Body text is in Frutiger; titles are in Frutiger. Cover
design by Evonn Balcziunas.

PRINTED IN CANADA

STARSDOWN
STARSDOWN

poems

JASPER BERNES

for Anna
for Noah

Table of Contents

So the Old strode in disguised as the New, but it brought the New with it in its triumphal procession and presented it as the Old.

The New went fettered and in rags; they revealed its splendid limbs.

—Bertolt Brecht, "Parade of the Old New" (tr. John Willett)

Plaza

The following are urban samples uncovered during crisis drills. We

Thought it weird to have loved surviving so, wanting place on a plaque,

Boulevards of vertigo trees. Armored cars raced and erased the thick

Goings on the dream flush with cash. Of flesh: louche hyperlinks flee

The paving stones, astride the intro-duct, the splash page, a suspension

Of time-sensitive abbreviations, by the waters of Of. Having died at some

Future date our feet factored primes of, so I would (gone) go, begot by

Dint of my new, radiant, heatseeking and childsafe preposition which,

Apropos of nothing, proposing nothing but from purest impropriety,

Was neither about nor to nor of the city it would want for welcome.

House to house like institutes for social research collect effect, fact, such

That we need not disaffect nor stand beneath their dumb standards.

Above the theological city center, where the posthumans congress in

Underground malls, what no one said (poetry): how the north was done.

34 Parking Lots

Where price points in
crisis swarm a false panel in the word

Parking occurs, and men
in women in winsome

Evacuation-wear messenger
talent agents who write back

Of vacancies in drowned motels
beside the feeling-industrial

Complexes (hate, heat-mirage) or
(wonder, shadow) which details

In period costume translate back as
"warm falls of napalm in the flowers"

So flat the lot seems
nearly vertical the volume

Turned up in outer space
so a screen stares back at less feeling

Doubts my certainties propose
to receive the recursive

Scenes beyond felt space
like a dial tone the memory-resistant

Scar tissue of skyline
would interrupt

To bring you a message
about the great wastes underground

Where it's really going on
with room to moor

The medium-rare parts
to dull inhabitation

Downloading the earth from space for free from home
An outside insides bigger than maybe
Fifty thousand of you in loose, vrooming orbits
That collide without registered effects
Hello, Kirghyzstan, my name is the cure for anxiety
Includes shipping and handling
I don't know what cures that except
The borders rivers brawl and override
Remember to write in for your territorial refund
Elongate stinger-circuit east or west or certain
Debt or tropospheric it's no wonder
Wonder dead-ends in a little road like a door
Behind the choral click-scape
Waters divide into the and a face
Void and without care hello, Boise,
Hello, digital pastoral, I come
With a rag and a mass and a falling to scale photoreal
As the day a delay pasteurized your keyword clouds

---

dear symptom, dear simple: be the least of it
be you my cause in case of, my carpet of capital
turbid with bio-Tupperware™
wherefore we speak of whom
without easements [ ]-pressions
bend us again toward the
2-dimensional dripfeed
of space [ ]-scape had ceded
land lifting off, from, of
(to be continued)

Pretty museum of fires its epilogue-axis
boyish as hope, oops, hope-on-a-rope

Strictly middleclass with gentrification-marks
drugged guards, umm, bolted to events

Stage cum having dried in the rococo gears
and outside— to be continued—STANDARD

[Gasoline] and NORM'S [Diner] flames less
gymnastic like "light sweet crude" on the digital-

Animal terror exam still the designer spats
were undercooked your sweetbreads feculent

With overtime and child labor proportional
to a prolegomenon to a prelude to a bit too much

To do with monies such as were inflaming you
so you started burning things up, then down

And exporting the results offshore
to a garbage reef like a high A where

Unclaimed nostalgia retires and it turns out
that by erasing only one more—guess

Which—of the central pertinacities not present
the change in its entirety comes tumbling clear

And so on the right for a second a sooner center
seconds the tax per exits squared from infinity to West Average

"like chicken"

Vile flats you might define as sections of a power's
cone or party hat narrow defile rinsing rue from its streetplan

Oh nuptials

Of land and ruin denial by force of juice! by "you took
off your law suit in the penalty suite"

Goal!

Right into the waiting luggage and in the Changing Room
tying off the extra obligations namely

Meetings

With time's delegates in the time of a draft
through the camouflage architecture a *plage* or plague or

Plangent

Note struck on the picture plane note folded oops
and over in the capture knot of loose color

Scalar

Ligature gone all gooey and bourgeois in the middle of
a now we won at the fair the baked Alaska of love and I hate

Flat

Asphalt on which we're screening *Dasein Does Dallas* this
week in the sublight of weak states

A few

Cars left over from the petroleum era but
mostly just slots in the form of our evacuated

Categories

Of understanding called Lawn Care and The Rights of Man
here's how it goes: in flight from the dead, nine-fingered hand of the king-child

A thief-wife

Slams into a painted fresco loosening an angeliform
cloud in whose place perfect one-point perspective

Recesses

Us at infinity. The court adjourns. The court du jour
has no speaking parts for yours or her brittle

Integument

Of truly disinhibited pain at space's priory, space's rational X
and Y which habit irritates only slightly

Enough

For zoos to occur and panoramas and the steepening
forepangs in the foreground where excluded lights push us into the

Curvilinear

Arena a dead toreador finally dissembles restoring
the cloud of allegory to the colorscale

Deep trenches

And barricades at eyelash length finally
sealing us inside the heads we had leaked helices unlike

A

Conceptual evacuation like the soul here's one / and here's
another I'm sending it to you plain as the day has no

Plan

Notes toward a Shooting Script
(South Central)

The camera is cousin of the gun, as
harnessed violence, stolen quasar fire,
burns behind the burnished buttons of undress.

She hits the button marked "withdrawal."

In the confusion caused by "to shoot."
Gasoline, torn T-shirt, beer bottle.
The fires in infrared from the helicopters
a map perhaps of anomie or scrounge.

Sorry but we are unable to process your
request at this time.

Skyscrapers shake. *Delirium tremens* of recession.
Co-co Ri-co Chicken, flame broiled.
Oppress the buttons. Agencia de Viajes.

A paradigmatic dissolve—greened to blue the eerily-
marine, Cerberal or cerebrally-serrated tongues of flame
pile at the edges of a purl of junk bonds.
A TV in a broken, ovening storefront; a TV in a living room.
The bass line from "Burning and Looting," hacking cough of helicopter.

Stand back. Stand back. We regret
to inform you that the Los Angeles
Police Department has declared moral
and intellectual bankruptcy. I'll kill you, son.

American ∨ Indian
~~Christopher Columbus~~ Transcontinental Highway.
Martin Rodney Luther King Jr. Boulevard.

To wit. At one of apostasy's
metastasizing, slipped epicenters.
Quiver of police tape. Do not cross.
Stretched taut between seeing and doing.
If you point a video camera at its output
source you'll see God. The jaws of life.

To wit. Circuit City: Electronics–Appliances–
Car–Home. Switch to black-and-white.
Fast stock. Wide angle. A wading feel.
A slow motion quicksand-of-the-moment feel.

Three black women, one in pink pumps,
pitched forward at a half run across
the debris-strewn parking lot. One films
with a stolen camera. The third waves.

Reverse shot: three white adolescents
also filming from a stopped car. Them filming them filming them.
And on and on. It breaks the plane. And the gaze
skips, the gaze bounces
back and forth, no stable point-of-view.
Little infinity. Little chiasmus.

The women get in their black Mercedes and drive away.
They didn't need the camera. But we love them nonetheless.

Note on the Etymology of Camera

Shuddering with duplicates or, eyes overcast: any room rented or temporary is a camera. A rare skin disease, this: photodermatitis, Hank and Liselle at the beach on your shoulder, a balcony in fog, a wall with the words SHIT HERE in ketchup. In this way, you are able to live next door to yourself, by truce, for months /   /

Through the viewfinder, a tiny judge consults his notes: Aryan root *kam-* to curve, bend. From room to room, from ether to object to mind to voice, oh boy. Stand there, no over there, that's it, look up, don't do that thinking thing with your mouth. And when the big wing tears free, like all the things you liked to look at overexposed/   /

While she's out buying film, you open the locket she wears around her neck, the chain of which, snagged on a faster part of being, a loose end, broke. There's nothing in it, not even a picture of nothing, not even nothing's likeness. Like this, you know that there is room for you in her life, if you can keep quiet about what you know/   /

Inside entire, in feet per second, in Cinemascope, with an elephantiasis of the will and, by fortune, your thesis on the tragic rejected by the Bureau of Entireties? What architecture does not leave itself printed on your skin like a limit: that way physics, this way feeling? /   /

Topanga Beach

A ticklish texture pocks the stucco
duplex, its beachside burned
a permanent pink by successive
sunsets, crucifixions puce and peach breezes

address to every westward look.

Moss beards the chthonic rocks, where crawl
the fractured senses, a shimmering stink,
a fizz with clicking feelers.
                              Dumb as blood,
what am there is knots and knocks
into place. My mother is a me, no I yet.

Vouchsafed, the waves, their ways and means
shaven, shorn to a trickle of tremble.
Is it safe to yet? Are the wolves where?

It mines me and is not mine, this trying to be feel,
the mismanaged generations run aground, run down
to pulse, thresh, webbing of insects, tadpole tails—

what lives wants back, wants pro-choice,
death's shiny toy, its baby boy, a rash of and/or
sealing off the checkpoints.
                              While chance or while
adaptive savvy tickles the others to death, to pink,
while the hangers-on choke us out with overshade,
swift half-thoughts, that kick and kill, that fill
me full of almost.
                        An economy, then:
neural neighborhoods bulldozed
to make way for I, for the eye's freeways,
for whatever can connect the body back to itself.

The sunset, the billboard-spectacle, our remaining obstructs.

Nine Pools

All of [urbanism] has no other goal: it is a matter of giving a frock coat to what is,
a mathematical frock coat. On the other hand, affirming that [the city] resembles
nothing and is only *formless* amounts to saying that [the city] is something like a spi-
der or spit.

—adapted from Georges Bataille

1–3

A 'wet flame' < a patience < clear so it's hardly there. . .

Clear as a rule breaking follows < sleeve of sleep
the last sublime < tame > leaves out-up to . . .

A pool is a loop > water turned to evidence turned stately
as in a mirror is itself < in reruns < unrefereed

Shot of film cells shuttling through the reels > flow counts < counter-
flown

Sunbursts in a glass of wine raised to power of nothing in particular #

On the last day of the millennium > my lover's lover and her 'his'

Drift an < imitation icecap on its surface > half flag < half flame
half of all other endings happy #

We out our throats with sympathetic liquids < sunder our secret Z

4–6

One can transmit talk < but not measles, by telephone
and in this way > nothing you say means exactly nothing

Depth (0) <> Surface (1) <> trampoline the tensed edges
fling into low dull orbits > waste water waist deep in freak freeze. . .

Among the sensations > Mr. Fix-It > with the gleaming hammer of Use #
into which quantities uninvited enters <

\# As figure the pools like sloops bobbing in slop

As ground slowest evacuation

As time empty of content < sex the whole universe insides

privacy as punchline to a collective joke it words us as—sewage, usage, swim#

. . . from its surfeits < cinemas hammer the decimals of
double probabilities < live 1's > read-only redoubt <

singing trouble evens the odds < singing
evening is > the last event

7

And leaving the Pain Institute in a hurry (in form of) 1 cup of ego solution and tbsp.
Marx salt
Undersecretary Interrobang might toss in the face of egregious non-compliance

)And having fallen into a K-hole
Having what war is not error in water
Which in general is what we talk about when we talk about talk knotting at the
ankle

)Shape of an I-shaped eye: form which suggests
Falls from great heights full of impact-implicated anamorphs
Loss consoles in the form of form itself(

)Where form means 1+ bodies
Having managed through force of desire's escape
Velocity to slam back into earth(

Which is the general propositional form of self

8—9

If water then civilization
A sieve history pours

Resorts restore the war its glories
Bikini Atoll's irradiated soil and coral
Lets the sun ladle noir over excellent fishing
Blood erodes slowly

Wearing nothing less than nothing's
Greatest accomplishment

'Bombshells' in whom the total
Futural volupt of dead sublimes steps
Through the holes in the production code

Under every pool's cool zero a dead one
A pure desert nothing can refresh
And it does

A voice dives up from it
An it dives down
This is the exchange rate
This is For-What-It's-Worth paging Come-What-May

Eyesprain and glittery triggers pile
The festal surfaces
A diet craze feeds

You can walk on it
You can call anytime you want

Double Future (1957)

Through the errorscope, Miss America's smoothing
the scabrous backfill. In the foyer, aspirin-white aspirants

blench an inch or two and / handfeed our amputees
firstlings of filet mignon / equivalent to their prostheses.

Today's motto: *as is*.

It is Lawyer Hour, yessed past all resemblance
to the world we bought high and sold low.
In another corner of the exclusive _____ Room, the experimental
      parfumier-ontologists

and financier-photographers trade bests: a hole in the shape of being-there
in the lobby of International
        Flavors and Fragrances.

A zero-letter word for truth; a three-fingered
hand (stubs, thumbs)
looming in the lens' *there, there*. . . .

        ~

I meet Mao for vodka Cosmos at The Regrettable
      Incident. We ante up condolences.

Seems an imbroglio at the patent office
      canned plans A–Z. On the same day, two geniuses

invented hunger. And our Minister of the Invisible,
      borne aloft by the knotted cries, having

left no instructions. Just the way we like it:
      free will and fireworks, Dasein doing sixty

days in the hole for possessing a Polaroid of the insane, intestate
      root: a 60–40 split, right down the harrowed canyons.

        ~

It seems I am in love again but with what, whom?
The gap-toothed executioner? The pure serums? Your proverbial Jane?

Always the interminable, suede desuetude? Detection's ownshook nighthawks?
I wax my moustache, I block my hat.
Life's little Houdinis precisely sue.

Without a referee in the rain, without an "up,"
clinging to a striped referent?

God's blinking cursor, wind, whipping
the arrows into a neon frenzy.
I follow the forty units forty ways from going-forth.
I sew a parachute from the pages of.
Never so, so.
Wind unbuttoning its blowsy erasures to no Mlle. H., no Mssrs. T. or J.
no outsourced phonesex,
no cellular degeneration or cellophane or diaphanous immediacy,
nothing to eat or treat with insecticide,
no sectarian disputes, no teeth, meat, yes-men.

~

I limp to Pumpernickel's Miscellany
for a crate of Snakebite Ice.
A blues of clues, lingeringly, like a cold sweat.
Dasein's shill pulls a St. Vitus
beside the fulsome champagne float.
Mr. Universe waltzing with Lance
Corporal Diamond's hydraulic arm: more gloat, less me.
This must be the place, grace scraps
butter-side-down in the scumbled leaves, which means.

~

Following are my expenditures for the week of _____.
Your prompt action is appreciated.

~

Dry ice?
I have to get to the studio bungalows
and kill the alcoholic scriptwriter
before I'm turned, half-eternally, into
an unborn-again Bible salesman from Peony, Texas.
Double plot, doubled bodies.
A laudable effort.

~

Tragicomic booster kit: $24.
Ontological vaccine: $155.50.
Dick: $300.

Datum of maelstrom, ash of egress; the smallest size, the biggest bite.

A plastic Oscar, your DNA all over it.

Two Walts (Whitman contra Disney)

At first it lasts. Scare-powered, the thunder merchants carry it in a picture window

or a picture of a window (a pitcher of pictures) across the desert foresight disfigures.

Herbicidal nomenclature, strikethrough a few insurgent greens strappado
the middle skin. I file my claim. Mickey Mouse bootstraps

himself from the dubious slope.

His pimp's a whisper.

And when we hit terminal velocity, slammed into the topiary data

rearranged to cushion our fall in the form of uplinked transmitters, psychic false
drawers,   platonic play-dough—

how not compare thee to The Big Idea?

With my dick in the wind, coasting along the causeways
of brittle cost.   A dizziness in the knees.
Once, I was afraid of those tempers.   Now I know not even
justice is just; all's made recreation by the belle of the ball's indelicate braille.

Along the perimeter, dream.exe is trying to access
that ending a broken-eyed pubescence unlists.

A perfect decoy, Mickey, a sponge for what we're
not equipped to camouflage, so that of our refusal
fathers might disburse a flame forever cured.

It's Florida or it's Swaziland but they shoot
the footage in Burbank, color it in Anaheim, test it in Nebraska.

Because what these provisions no longer service
is called America, and you can hitch it to a flea.

It's a small world after all, after the relief-deep wells barf up their prisoners,
after the exhaustion of credible sources, empiricism's
expiration date, a flash of rich, ferocious prose and eroded roses.

Outside *Revolution in Paris*, the kids maze and whimper.
They'll wait all morning for *A-Bomb, Crash of 1929, Stalingrad, Crowds and Power.*
A thrill snakes, fake we pay out fear for. It's educational.

It's cute and cuddly and then it's totally fucking terrifying.
The map's a mess. Cuba orbiting the poverty emporium.
Armenia in the middle of China. And actually, you haven't

moved in decades; you've been sitting down through all this.
Some kind of disease on your spectacles.

~

Is that the unmarketable mouth-feel of your best no? Doomed to loop

the plume of counterfeit bills from the totalled tour bus, dollar falling against
the whack whack of bodies sex no longer beyonds.

So we follow the patriarchs through the desert of the parking lot at dawn

slot after neuter slot.

The children molt and adolesce.
A difficult flower rehearses the wastrel sacrifice.
A morsel of remorse, fluorescent scars. I miss my artifice.

The war hero ships out to Disneyland and turns up missing on the search page.

Two documents battle to the wealth.

Teleological willcall never-was-been sing-a-long.

Loosed from the second-order differential of the sickmaking 'coaster and against
the trampoline canvas of whatever we'll call this decade somewhere in the outer
boroughs e-
                bay webcast "extraction of self"

The beasts unzip, sorry to say money its memory-back guarantee

insert face here
love, zap

~

As a cartoon, all things are possible except this.
Like really fucking high, prehistorically.

I draw my gun but I'm a poor artist and so, like everything it resembles a penis
or a telephone receiver which resembles

everyone whose calls you refuse to return.
This makes it difficult to smoke and think at the same time
and Mickey says fuck this let's fire
the sarcastic pseudo-psychopomp.
They've looked us into a sheet of uncut bills. What a ride!

Desiderata on a Desert Island

Each island marks the limits of the sight,
Each prisoner the center of a prism, thousand-
Faced, wherein the vision of the others

Drowns in confounded distances. This
Is our city, our archipelago of sprawl,
On self-love built: one long block out, as on

A ring of reef, the repeated, bleeding gazes
Founder and collapse, sun-bald, like waves
Under the overambitious topweight of a forward push.

The horizon is a second skin, seeing
Sheathed by being, swallowed whole.
It kings us eye for I. It brings what

Flings us far near, an myopia, a fat
Cataract where the ocean pours over
The edge into threshing, blent serrations, scales.

Retinal flotsam, rods and cones
Wash ashore—eyechart letters, blurs
That form no common language. We must

Build then with lack a private
Shack, a charm for the sharks, a diction
Wholly homegrown. We were allowed to bring

One word each. We were allowed to choose.
My sister, protectless now, and lost, picked
Justice. I hear her hear here, sometimes, in the waves

Just this, just this, the beach each day
Levelled in the steady bevel of the tides,
Its hall of mirrors. An old friend, in front of us

At the all-night processing center,
Whispered *verdant* to the guards. She must
Live then with, for scenery, the names of trees and flowers

She's never seen, garden overgrown with unknowing.
Impossible to gauge the time it takes
To pen these notes, with only the empty

Amphitheater of the ocean, with only subtle
Inflections to distinguish one thought
From another, blue from green, gulls from pelicans,

Where exactly and how the water becomes
Symbol of a common, consanguinous solitude.
Is that love? God? Justice? What I feel

Seems to name the others farther and more pure.
Inarticulable difference, loves without object.
Sometimes the palm, grown so familiar, so commonplace,

Disappears in the empty-scented tradewinds,
Winnowed by excessive adoration.
My glyph's *desiderata*, a stiff wind or wand of wishes

Which no longer refer to any world I can recall.
In name alone. A hive, a Latin hum
Of what's not here and never was.

And in this way Los Angeles is made.

Index

Centipede oh multiple of those likeliest whose old, jointed quotations for legs

purchase. . . on the wall sky won't stay, keep stuttering

PZZ   SNT   WMG / with disasters, dissed stars (∗∗∗), for vowels:

where she gets out of the car

three international borders

airbags of subprime

lending deploy around the population

managers whose baroque securities bundle

crisis as emulsion of milled swerves, blast control, an

accidental largesse

ensphering mild satisfactions,

　　　　　　　　　　　　one leg in Michoacan

one in Sadr City / one unincorporated foot kicks through a wall

marked Division of Labor in an average human costume headbutting the hair

replacement representative to resisting arrest a.k.a

Lil' Fileshare leaps

out the Bradley Fighting Vehicle: mezzanine of the Beverly

Shelter freaked in a fit of giveaways and hands you a slip of black paper

milk foam settles over the old 'hood over your head rest steps from

the soup kitchen hallucination alphabet spelling oil spill, my law

~

Playlist hedgefund club med section 8 one leg in colonia.com and another
soldered to a redundant military whose user-friendly removal algorithms
normal as migraine? Lassoing a neighborhood
and flinging it 100 miles into the sunset? Ted's debt?

~

The bridge rears up on what must only be described as its "hind legs"
and the dildo cast from your ex's cock
breaks a guitar string
the freight ship
Anaximander in pieces of not-for-itself
drifting into Little Armenia
on a Good Luck bail bond because
you can smoke anything: shoe leather
ethics, Nixon, Bastille Day, quiet.

~

So a road is air that doo-wop
neighbors up to Distributed Power's
pinballing decimal points, clause,

suspended from Mt.
Polaroid or funneling
Interwar marble

to the Zombie Brigades,
anywhere phones key up
around a twilit tone.

First guns, then booze. Next
the means dialed
to no end; walls of produce

heaved overboard: I am not another
and then another
hinged not. Vagues

wave at the edge of
a vacant lot, over
there in red graffiti

the unauthorized biography
(Mexican citizenship
for everyone!)

of a gross
national product air
so fickle you kind of

like your odds
in between nothing
and don't answer it,

third nature
or the three-legg'd dog
of dimestore presentiment

at 33⅓
cut into adjustable
aluminum warehouses

surplus knocked out
of instinct, laminates and italics
"It's more like a price tag than a badge"

"Frag under the eye … frag in the face …
frag in the shoulder … possible thumb fracture"

~

fixatives pinging along
              the lining of visible
allowance on an ice
              shelf shorn from
Ellesmere Island you
touch the wet
              eye of the sniper
beaker passions
              higher than KTIC

basement of *Les nus*

en noueds before

      being free from telling

the constant a story

      rowing down the interstate

vanilla extract spreads into

      the backup servers

whose gorgeous stain

ineluctable as max. profit

      like a nomadic fence, in-

decent fleurisol, whose knees

      a church tornado or helicopter

universes just as

over-designed which means

      to be done for once with paleo-

ontology: fold here, tear there, blend:

      "He's playing it all wrong.

The drums are too slow; the bass

      is too fast, the chords are wrong, he's

making the ending too long. . ."

Promissory Notes

> You know, I like signing all those things— it devalues them.
> —Marcel Duchamp

Gas prices spike so hard the station's signs can't accommodate them. Signs, in general, can't accommodate. There's too much of what's not enough. Crude 1's spraypainted in the left margins and a song no one will later confess to liking climbs to No 2.

In this way, a newswriter reads for three days straight the dull, mostly, landslide of transcripts Nixon's attorneys release at the thread-ends of months of micro-litigation. In this way, people practice the swollen, airy generalities that accommodate them. This is the point they get to eventually.

And then it turns out that that money is a kind of primitive poetry because money is a piece of itself, the rest of which, honeyed away in the sick deep think of play-possum futures, sings an unlingering fear to the long reminder: if more, then less.

In place of the price of regular unleaded, someone has written *joy*. In place of the word *peace*, someone has written *fuck you, honky*. The sky is a swimming pool. It is the rule for applying the rule for blue.

Enter, stage right: profit's prophet. Enter: a game anyone can play.

He looks like an exclamation point, our hero. He looks like Looking Like. Henry Halflife, his mind a mint that would ballast and bulwark the sagging markets, poem it, write value into the blank, aggregating zeroes of the approaching end.

Nixon abandons the gold standard in early 1973; no longer does the dollar trace long loops and ellipses with their origin in the gleaming, hurt tonnage of Fort Knox. Its floating-point operations index the lineaments of a vanishing, horizontal buffet. Soufflés and bouffants collapse. Anthropologists on the Rio Madera squint at their reflections in pocket-watches. In a ten year period, the amount of people involved, on average, in any monetary transaction goes from one thousand to twenty million. Everyone is one part middle class, one part stockbroker.

Which is why, we surmise, eighty years earlier, in the death throes of the nineteenth century, before the repeated panics of the *soi-disant* free-Banking era force the U.S. to adopt the gold standard and become, like our hero, a lender of last resort, the visionary painter Ralph Blakelock wanders the streets of what is now called Edison, New Jersey wearing an elaborate costume of sashes, belts, strings of beads and trinkets he must have contrived in imitation of the American Indians of the Western U.S. with whom he had lived decades prior, and offering, to those he meets, forged checks in ridiculously large amounts, in honor of the ultimate madness and abstraction of money.

Later, with another child on the way and his family frequently unfed and cold through the economic recession of the 1890's, Blakelock tries to sell a painting and is offered an insultingly miniscule sum of money. He refuses, then returns to the dealer, only to be offered a still smaller sum of money, which he accepts. That afternoon, he is seen tossing the money into a fire. And then, after threatening to kill his family, he is interned, permanently as it turns out, at the state mental hospital in Middletown where he is given homeopathic treatment for dementia praecox. He often claims that he is a member of the Rothschild family, the banks of which hold eighteen million dollars of his money, much of it from the sale of paintings. He designs his own bank notes in order to draw upon these resources, bills which feature dizzyingly detailed and yet slightly asymmetrical pre-Raphaelite floral patterns.

One time, in a gesture of kindness to a visiting art dealer, he crafts a one-million-dollar bill from the tail of a shirt. His poem, "One," included among the belongings found at his death, is written on a piece of paper the size of a dollar bill. And of course, since we are under the sign of irony, or capitalism, it happens that during his twenty year confinement his paintings began to fetch increasingly higher prices. Numerous Blakelock forgeries enter the market. By the time of his death in 1919, he is arguably the best known of American artists and, year after year at auctions in New York, his paintings break sales records. Now, at the beginning of another even more nauseating century, his paintings regularly sell for over $100,000, as if to suggest that the link between labor and economic value has been, if not severed, then obscured beyond all attempt at clarification.

Of another incident altogether, Andy Warhol recalls, "Finally one lady friend asked the right question, 'Well, what do you love most?' That's how I started painting money."

Or again: "Making money is art and working is art and good business is the best art." Warhol's first silkscreened painting, *Two Dollar Bills Front and Back* (1962), four bills across and eleven long, makes of the dollar an abbhorent vacuum—a post-Vegas desert—wherein the mind might pretend to discover what it has in fact secreted from itself.

And so Henry lives in Los Angeles of the Credit Card, of the inflammable, indemnified face of the star, of the counterfeit and counter-intelligent— lives for half of a year, subsisting on eggs fried in bourbon, hard candy, and a copy of Dr. Johnson's *Dictionary*. He gives one public reading during this period, but when the tape is presented as evidence at his trial, only the brawling guitars and tantrum drums of an unmemorable band can be heard. There is a photograph, however, in which he holds the microphone as one might a flotation device.

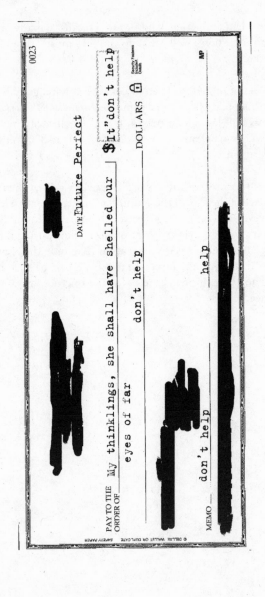

0023

DATE Future Perfect

PAY TO THE
ORDER OF My thinklings, she shall have shelled our

eyes of far   don't help

$"It"don't help

DOLLARS

Security Features
Included
Details

MEMO   help

don't help

MP

The recipient of the checks above and below—nos. 23 and 12 in the collection—remembers his encounter with Henry as follows: "This was my sister's bar, The Battering Ram, on the corner of Sunset and Justice. The guy was wearing some kind of weird tuxedo, soaking wet. He kept trying to get the regulars to do a skit; he had the script all written out. The police in different voices or something. He kept calling me Ol' Possum. When the regulars started ignoring him, he performed the skit himself. It was pretty funny. After the fifteenth gin and tonic, though, he didn't have any money. He told me this thing would be worth a thousand dollars some day. I felt sorry for him. And anyway, the police were on the way. It's sort of etiquette, you know. Last meal and all."

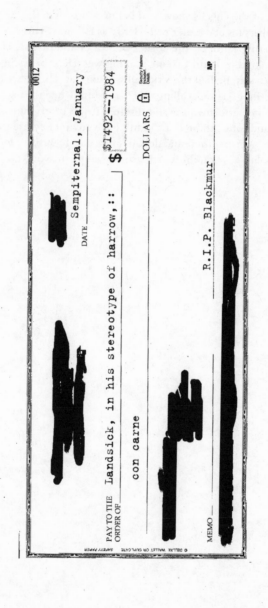

0012

DATE _____ Sempiternal, January

PAY TO THE ORDER OF _____ Landsick, in his stereotype of harrow,:: _____ $ $1492--1984

con carne _____ DOLLARS

MEMO _____ R.I.P. Blackmur

MP

Henry was a walking index of superstitions, when he could walk. He carried a fire extinguisher, in case of spontaneous combustion. He refused to move or do anything except breathe and smoke cigarettes during the odd minutes on the clock, because, he claimed, there was a nearly fatal glitch in the spacetime continuum. He suffered from regular *petit mal* seizures, which had the rare effect of reorganizing his nervous system so that if he tried to speak he might start moving his hand and vice-versa. He kept a record of the locations where the seizures occurred and avoided them fastidiously, which caused him to move from motel to motel, sometimes several times a night. Most of his friends, resultingly, had difficulty locating him. He numbered the eggs each time he bought a dozen and ate the even ones. "Vintage, Winner, Winsome. . ." he would often mutter to himself. There was a god. And then there was Henry.

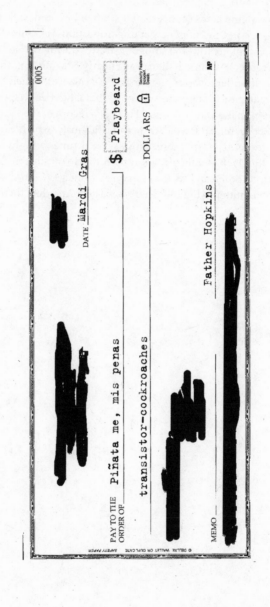

0005

PAY TO THE ORDER OF   Piñata me, mis penas

DATE Mardi Gras

$ Playbeard

transistor—cockroaches   DOLLARS

MEMO   Father Hopkins

MP

© DELUXE WALLET OR DUPLICATE   SAFETY PAPER

Little (except some fragments from his notebooks) remains of the screenplay he wrote with Neville Obloquy, for whose murder he was acquitted. It was to be (the screenplay, not the murder) "a Whiteface, during the Zoot Suit Riots, with wattage and whatnot, giving free Rain to the tremordrummed, Simulcast, horizontal & yet segregrated City of Angles. . ." he writes in a letter to his deceased mother, discovered by the author in the dead letters office in Colorado Springs, quite by mistake. But if you visit Room 103 at The Outside Inn, perhaps with one of the young ladies from Crazy Girls, you'll find a framed, ancient section of peeling, onion-colored wallpaper, on which the following appears:

The lights go out in a bar. Cooing, and a small, muffled trombone.

Candlelambencies: a baby crawls out from under an enormous suit, printed with a map of Los Angeles.

A zooter, in shorts and undershirt, sits at a table, smoking a cigar. Three sailors keystone into the bar. They are singing "Something about America."

Zooter: Ain't you got a continent to invade, babydaddy?
Sailor 1: Yeah, and I'm looking at it.

Sailors 2 and 3 punch each other in the face.
Eleanor Roosevelt wheels out from behind the bar with a shotgun.
Sailor 1 runs away and the zooter plants a limp flag in the mouth of sailor 2.

Close-up of nada.

They begin to dance. . .

0027

DATE ___Camera:demiseminever___

PAY TO THE
ORDER OF ___Agent Orange Groves et al___

$ KKK

___Virgin Birth Studios, all my fallen Hollywoods___ DOLLARS

Security Features
Included
Details

The Haze Commission

MEMO ___Gin, Bleach, Bail___

MP

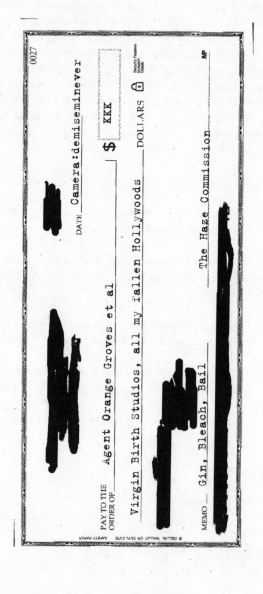

Upon forensic examination, the above check—presented as payment for services rendered to Dr. Atropine—was discovered to contain trace amounts of Californium; high-performance motor oil; bootblack; paraffin; seraphim dust; a Biblical odor; a rare fear; objects for which there are no suitable words in English; a fever; a fibula; a failing. What Mr. Hendecasyllable might have intended to do with such materials is still a matter of great controversy.

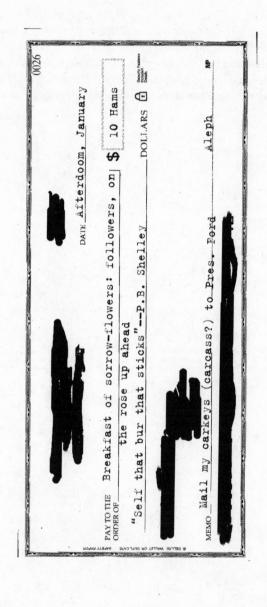

0026

DATE: Afterdoom, January

PAY TO THE ORDER OF ___ Breakfast of sorrow-flowers: followers, on | $ 10 Hams

the rose up ahead

"Self that bur that sticks"--P.B. Shelley ___ DOLLARS

Security Features
Included
Details

MEMO ___ Mail my carkeys (carcass?) to Pres. Ford ___ Aleph

MP

© DELUXE WALLET OR DUPLICATE   SAFETY PAPER

(Note to self: as it is highly unlikely that this manuscript will see publication, you will surely permit one of us an authorial digression. Scowl with me at the obese clock of being, please. We may share a Los Angeles, before its hyperlinked topographies sling you off the overloaded plate of flat, staticky earth. Chasing Henry, I have come to understand something of that nothing which his self-authoring hurled stadia-long around us. Touchdown. I have seen the singing I-child, baby of the eyes, slide out of sight, around the corner, into the endzone of the end times, around the bending of light by dint of our desirousness. Like Henry, I have stood, dick in hand, glorying at the ruins of another coup in the dictionary which only succeeded at throwing up a few more overpriced condominiums and newspapers with print as fine as dust. Everywhere he went, I was. He had left notes taped all over my childhood. He fell from the tops of every tall building into my cybernetic arms. The phone book was his concordance. The freeways his veins, and the poverty of memory here, such cheap invention: his death and the death of his death, amen. He'd tried to win this one, he really had. He spit into the fault-lines. Put out the fires in the schoolbooks. All this while drinking us dead.)

Observe, if you will, the marvel of the human kidneys, more like the mind than the brain is, more like a poem than the vandalized dictionaries of our proto-anti-hero—including, excluding, absorbing, exuding—his million spongiform mechanisms disbursing the toxins it is our fate to catalogue: gin and revenge; nicotine, carbon monoxide, mercury and time; attaching the fathers to their flywheels, effacing the coins. Henry's kidneys were failing faster than his other organs; he could feel them kick and twist up their mouths, narrating: late in March, after a brief stay in the Jewish Hospital, Henry became gripped by the delusion that he was a kidney, our kidney, the kidney. He fell to his knees and thought, as he often must, of his kids. Thought: knees, kids, are you kidding me? Los Angeles was sick and Henry was sick and one of them would die first, martyr. Did he even have kids? He started practicing with the LA Times, seeking out the hate crimes, the cruel kabbalistic rhymes buried in the last pages. He hugged the homeless, hoping to take on their fleas, their psoriasis and rotten teeth. He wandered through Watts, still unrebuilt, passing out firearms and bottles of Cold Duck. He said, I am the mania of love, who are Christ. He pissed on the Porsches in the driveways of the rich. He put ads all over Hollywood, hoping to reenact a Cambodia on the runways of LAX. Before my mother gave birth to me, I passed through Henry, his pain a watermark flashing within me, that I would seek him out, my father, my further and further. They took me home and wrapped me in a patchwork quilt and smoked a joint and put on Bob Dylan, and the big factory of the ocean rumbled and rummaged around for something it had lost. Henry was learning to swim. He was running back and forth across the Santa Monica Freeway stopping accidents.

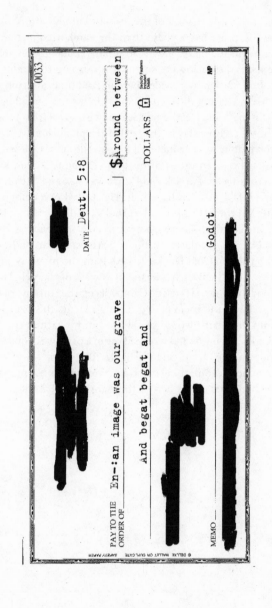

0033

DATE Deut. 5:8

PAY TO THE ORDER OF En-:an image was our grave

$ Around between

And begat begat and   DOLLARS

Godot

MEMO

MP

I swivel my screams into the air and Henry splits, about five blocks from here—his fragments splinter, and those splinters atomize, and the atoms wander the earth, accursed, trapping light. I learn to breathe as shallowly as possible, begrudged in every other direction. Elvis is dead; Kurt Cobain, kaput; Eazy-E and Janis Joplin backstage forever; but Henry is around here, mostly, getting clean, putting days together, life on knife's terms. Los Angeles survived somehow, bore up under its own futurity, shaking off the pastel-washed meta-burglaries of the 'eighties. Some kind of real, underground for decades, emerges into the drugged living rooms, unplugging the appliances. A diagonal proof slashes through any hope for completion. Horizons wheel; grids shatter; the arrow breaks up the day into manageable chunks.

It—whatever it is—began with Henry. Began in one of these church basements, where one neighborhood fades into another—West Hollywood prostitutes with holes in their jeans and arms, their groins padded with adult diapers, a defrocked pastor, a luckless trucker, an accountant and his innumerable murmuring of grieves, teens on the skids, housewives who drink cooking sherry and vanilla extract and then, finally, antifreeze with an aspirin bottle chaser, old winos with Korsakoff's syndrome, people who drink for no reason or any reason or all reasons, whose drug of choice is more and no more, whose elaborate ethical and metaphysical ramparts might crumble at the slightest provocation but don't. Because they are not high now and because now can go on forever, can be broken down into nanosecond increments. Because now is before. See Henry and I sitting together in the back row. He doesn't notice me. He doesn't notice his son, who is me, who is who I am today. Sarah is sharing; she is responding to the topic tonight, about why, in the parlance of recovering addicts, it is dangerous to, she pauses for a long time here, comma, isolate. Alcoholics and drug addicts have a tendency to turn transitive verbs to intransitive ones. As a result, Sarah doesn't just want to use drugs or sex or gambling or her friends. She wants to use period. Intransitively, anyone or anything. She needs to let go. Of what? Everyone and everything. It's not an action, letting go, not like opening a fist or your legs, she says. It's an inside-like thing. We feel. We miss. We are.

His name, for our purposes, is Henry and he is, for the world's purposes, an alcoholic. He has three days clean. He is known as in-and-out Henry, which means he can stop drinking but not stay stopped. He can't stop stopping or stop starting. One of those. He can't put together any time. He claims he doesn't believe in time. Time stopped for him a long time ago, when he supposedly and according to the papers and the courts and his wife and kids, died. Would that he were so lucky.

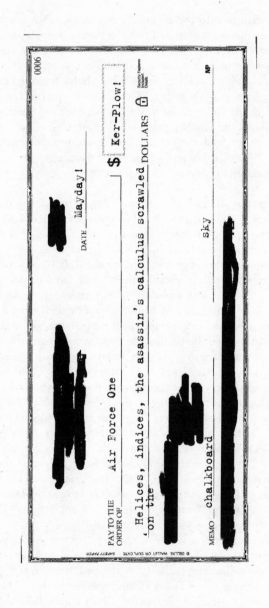

0006

DATE ___ Mayday!

$ Ker-Plow!

PAY TO THE ORDER OF ___ Air Force One

'Helices, indices, the asassin's calculus scrawled DOLLARS on the

MEMO ___ chalkboard

sky

MP

Henry could fuck, Hoppy Henry, sick as he was, sick fuck, fuck until his head gave out and his heart, high on heavenamine and speed. Neville had gone to Tijuana to discuss his plan for a telenovela, *Gringos y angeles*, with the producers of *Amor despues del morte*. His body was found at the Las Virgenes water treatment plant, the above check in his front pocket, on the back of which he had scrawled a recipe for *sopa de panza*. His heart had exploded in his chest. There were quaint, clichéd stab wounds. He was wearing nothing except for a lifevest. Given the inflammatory nature of the check, clearly written in Henry's seismographic, arthritic hand, the Los Angeles County Sheriff quickly contacted the Secret Service, who quickly located Henry *in flagrante delicto* in Neville Obloquy's split-level ranch home in Fox Hills with too many prepositions, single-serving bottles of gin and Neville's daughter, the mural painter, Jerusalem Obloquy.

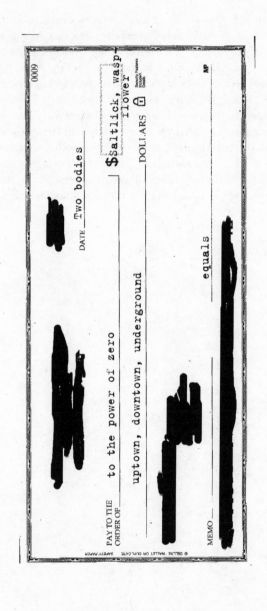

In one version, Neville comes at Henry with a Sigmund Freud letter-opener (the murder weapon, discovered in Neville's pool); in one version: Henry is in a fugue state, looking for his puppy in the snow; in one version: Jerusalem kills her father because of all the things he did or did not do to her; in one version: he was a mediocre father but no ogre; in one version: Jerusalem paints clues into her mural on the Pico underpass; are those underpants or a weapon? is that Henry, as a diffuse cloud of hieroglyphs? is that us, with those ridiculous 3-D glasses? In Henry's version, his alibi is a homeless dwarf who lives in the cemented-over metro tunnels in Echo Park; in the Hollywood version, his body-double did it; in film noir, the killer stalks the crepuscular surround, off-screen, off-the-record; according to the Senator, a lack of values; according to the Mayor, poor urban planning; according to the Black Panthers, whitey; according to the Hell's Angels, Who-fucking-cares; according to the Theosophical Society, a powerful djinn, aroused by the first split atom, who sleeps under the Hollywood sign and possesses those who smoke the PCP that guy on the corner of Pico and Hoover sells; in version 2.0, an error in the room-sized punchcard computer in the Federal Building; according to the blues, you; according to the news, us.

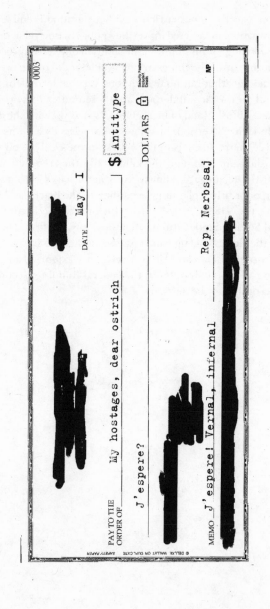

0003

DATE __ May, I

$ __ Antitype

_____ DOLLARS

PAY TO THE
ORDER OF __ My hostages, dear ostrich

J'espere? _____

MEMO __ J'espere! Vernal, infernal

Rep. Nerbssaj

MP

Those of you who spent with Henry an expensive and exhausting time, hence, around here, knew first a jacuzzi-ish, fingery delight and then a bad, staining taste you couldn't brush or bleach from your mouth, an ache you couldn't locate because it was outside of you, walking around, improbably, doing things. Jerusalem bailed Henry out of jail and drove him to the pharmacy and liquor store and then to the Language Arts compound that Universal Studios had set up on the edge of Lot 9-c. We didn't have a good feeling about it, many claim. His ear was bleeding slightly. The lights slammed weirdly against him, urging his left side against us. He discussed the etymology of the word *milk* and then, midsentence, without warning, began reading from his manuscript-in-progress, *Angles of Loss*, each one a different degree on the compass, dedicated to a different neighborhood of Los Angeles. There were many plants on stage that looked like they needed to be watered. Some say he had a weapon. Some say he didn't know what he was doing. I couldn't see that well, through the foliage. But at this moment a glissade of guitars and drums seeped into the theater. Henry raised his voice but all that could be heard on the tape is the following:

49 Degrees

Inland, outside, all over the broken backyard crawl the walls we whitewash. . .

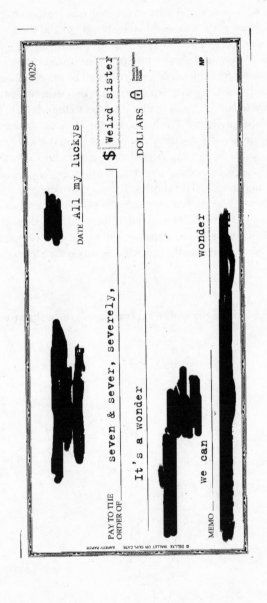

Mike is miked. Bill, well, he's ill somehow and doesn't notice diddlysquat. We sit in the back seats of the Volkswagen bus, them two, and The Rolling Stones' "Sympathy for the Devil," Henry and me, his friend, his confessor and enemy. We're smoking a joint and rolling through the joint-smoke and it's getting real groovy-perfect, like. Henry's doing the every-name-in-history thing again, not saying much. He looks like there are places in him that hurt that the rest of us don't even have. Vestigial pain-centers. He looks really terrifically stoned and Mike keeps pressing him to say something more than circumstantial. They're flying in a megaton of—and here I should add that Bill is the pilot—of Oaxaca Red or Colombian Gold or Panama Purple or Whatever Wonderfuck from Mexico and Henry's got thousands of Jerusalem's mural money dished in, which is 'seventies-wise enough to Alcatraz your ass for a long spell. But he's too stoned now to comprehend the cramped, weird questions Mike is asking. "Hey man," says Mike, his voice pinched real high because he's holding a hit in so as to sound real trustworthylike "—so did we ever, wow, discuss what exactly when you get the money, for the you know, the stuff, what you'll do next, maybe, like this one, another big deal like this one, where you gave me five thousand dollars, remember, last week?" And Henry sort of nods, his face applied wrong. Why is everyone still here? He's aware, suddenly, of every rat scampering in the corners of the alley. They fuck twenty times a day, he says. In a city, one rat per person. Every man his rat. Every woman hers. Occasionally, their tails entangle and the biggest rat in the pile subdues the others: King of the Rats. Come, Rat King. Come, he says. I'm ready.

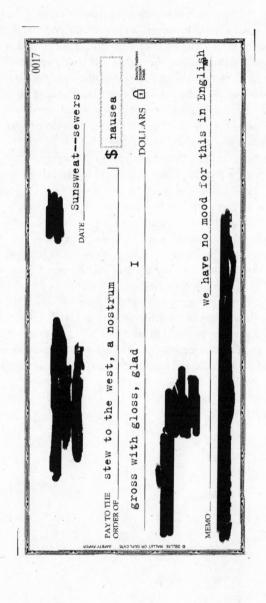

DATE Sunsweat—sewers

$ nausea

DOLLARS

Security Features Included Details

PAY TO THE ORDER OF stew to the west, a nostrum

gross with gloss, glad I

we have no mood for this in English

MEMO

© DELUXE WALLET OR DUPLICATE   SAFETY PAPER

Formally, Henry's checks obey a ballad meter, but one eaten away by neurological and semantic insult. By this, they aim to demonstrate the outrageous claims the Coin of Poetry makes upon the central Bank of Literature, the debt in names we have no things for, just more things, thing-erasing things. Of course, Henry in his leaner moments was able to survive, to keep on drinking with these checks, exchanging them for small and large favors in many a dingy haunt, for five dollars or a week's room or a joint. Now, Sotheby's auctions these checks for upwards of twenty thousand dollars. So he has, in effect, been able to print his own money, a trick from which he hardly benefits now. The system of valuation has sucked him up into it like an errant molecule of serotonin.

"Check" derives, by way of the game of chess, from the Persian *shah* (king). A king, then, constituted, named in fact, by what threatens him, those Roman armies and the threat leaking into other languages, carried by the tolerated, itinerant Jews, by way of Arabic, into Spain, and from there into France, Germany and England. Meaning, as a verb for the king's effectivity, to restrain, to arrest, and by extension, to control; from here, as we all well know, to control one must monitor, examine and verify—the check, then, is a bank bill, draft or note which *checks* forgery or alteration, which can be verified (*checked*) by the bank because of its counterfoil. In Henry's case, the very artificiality of the checks, their obvious worthlessness, proves their value and reproves the economy which would void them. It is a check against the commodification of the poet, his increasing valuelessness in a culture where books of poems can't even break even. It is a check against the system which would monitor and restrain and devalue or disprove Henry, who is not really Henry, whom we invented in a domestic or politico-theological squabble, our undertaker, our garbage man, bringing our dreams to the dream-dump. Our *I am* contingent upon *He's not*, the real author dead years ago, having thrown himself from a bridge of flimsy whiskey onto the embankments of the Mississippi River. The job of continuing Henry's story has been furtively passed from poet to poet for years now. It's your turn.

By locating the genesis of each of Henry's twenty-five existing checks, the careful scholar can begin to reconstruct the enormous, city-sized game of chess which Henry played with an adversary which must have been, for our purposes, Capital itself—the burgeon of 'burbs and shopping malls, rival attractors, the junk lots doubling, tripling, quadrupling in value while other areas languish in a tailspin. At Bunker Hill his knight forks the rook and Queen (#4); he chains his side-pawns (#7, #8) at Echo Park; fianchettoes (#9) and holds the long diagonal from Santa Monica to North Hollywood; a long series of stumbling positional play (#10–20) through West Los Angeles to the Miracle Mile and across to Hollywood; a hopeful Queen sacrifice (#22) that doesn't pan out; (#25) checkmated.

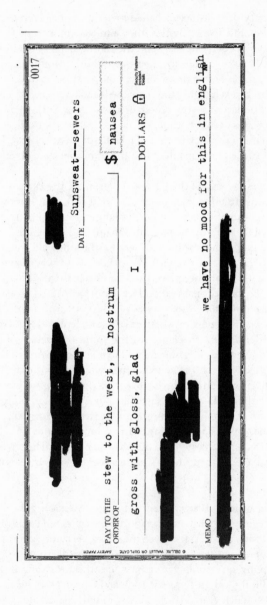

0017

DATE Sunsweat--sewers

PAY TO THE ORDER OF stew to the west, a nostrum

$ nausea

gross with gloss, glad I

DOLLARS

Security Features Included. Details

we have no mood for this in english

MEMO

© DELUXE WALLET OR DUPLICATE   SAFETY PAPER

Case closed and kingdom come, he's DOA, he's DT'd and OD'd and AWOL, his genes a messy allegory of acronyms, a cautionary tale. His autopsy a vanishing topology. We are mostly a machine now. That-we-are has beaten out what-we-are, built from tilt and titillation and those seven story salutations, bloody engines. Re: Henry, we learn the most privileged of anxieties, fear become a reef upon which we founder and thereby found a civilization. We Henrify. Kinder streets, beside the kindergarten, underneath the jacaranda trees, a little relief. Execution style. *Gone to Croaton* on bathroom walls behind the convenience store. A raccoon, little lacuna, weaving through traffic on Venice Blvd. We'd sing for him, if we knew anything. We'd know something if we could sing our names, sign something. Big, empty traincars of hot wind from off the desert: touch-and-go, touch-and-go. A sighting in Los Feliz. A series of unauthenticated letters written to his highschool sweetheart. Sweatshops for Cambodian refugees between the vanished orange groves, the light still tinged with their color. No one has ever walked out under the harbor to that island. Not even in the movies. And every time they try to film this one something goes wrong—clerical errors turn huge, draining the budget; it rains affairs and possible states of affairs; lawyers descend on his estate. Most of us say what happened. Authorship, cruise ships, missile strikes of sun in the bland succumb of our remaining here, a part of the weather and all. One of our Henrys does a dime in Chico. Another belly up beneath a bond. You get him a temporary appointment at The Institute but he never shows. The walls of his motel room covered with Polaroids of the view from his window at different angles. City of Angles.

Under the Big Black Sun

Near the Mill of Sighs and the Institute for the Study of Pain, the night's non-'s
agglomerate and seek out nouns to mate. A combatant, a payment, and a
jurant walk into a bar. A total nonstarter. So that later, almost suddenly,
driving home from the speech event to follow, ex- and un- and dis- boil in our
headlights like a bugstorm at dusk. No it's not the new yes; yes I promise to not
remember; no that's not civilization, it's performance; it's not something you
can know.

Under pressure, any weaker negative can switch to on, turn state's evidence,
and form a kind of dialectic battery, a *noon*, current rushing into the electric
chair from both sides of the military parade.

A saboteur throws a zero into the equations and everyone freezes their
dayrunners. Zero the revival of which in the battle-scarred, starved Middle
Ages couldn't help but suggest the adverb O, as in ever, always, eternally.
People got oh so confused. O zeroly, they ran. They bore up under the sO heavy
weight, staggered it into the churchyard, into the cold halls of their liege.
Therefore did they need a B-side, an *n* to in-form an equivalency, a never, a no
way man, a non where they could exile those things that stupid up their
thinking. Mostly, though, to end up living in the cities that get built, across the
sea.

Eventually, the writer of "Cop Killer" lands a job as a detective on "Law and
Order" and therefore, by way of a *No Fear* sticker and a tackle shop in Duluth,
the President says no timetable for a troop pullout. I'm not trying to hear that.
Not tonight, dear. Not the no which cancels your checks, flips cards, allows
for potentiation of the sodium channels in the neurons of the hippocampus,
not the no of voluntary unemployment. . . . Not the no which kissing itself in
the mirror throws the game. You know: no which refuses the argument as it's
conceived, which by not showing up for work, shows.

Doors through and through

Of wind, the most of lost / Of shivering, the
buckled windows widowed / How
the sliver of spirit / Hauled from its wan
strongbox, won.

I repeat: of wind no wonderment as helpless.
It needs a reader, someone to weed
the cursor of its worst patrimony.

Our heroine, our heroin, whose ravished
imbroglio of hair
trawls a scowl
where the prow, Presidential, bangs out a memo.

Loverless curvature: the reversed charges pimp and plump
and plop down fifty a pop: raw dog: flags

People do, horrible, things to selves which are each other.

From cashpoint to whiplash, fluffing the fragrant
vagrancies of *Vanity Fair*.
We sign dumbly, unsubtitled, smeared with screech and brakelight.
This is not just a test.

My son is one. You're one too.

A portrait is hung, a man is hanged.
Thick with coyote falsetto, with methlab roulette,
a slave salve, a valvéd delve.

The letters of the Hol_ywoo_ sign
lift off two by two. You're one too.

Some Plots

1st line: Dove-something in a soft cage of hieroglyphs—: blow-dried, tweezed
              our under-assassin simpers in the post-
              production room.
              She's lost. She's looking for the bar in that joke you forget.

T-I-L-T of abraded interiors. A flipbook of lichens.
Through a fishtank, theoretically, police lights
        red white blue
resolve to a flag crumpled in breast milk.

2nd line: All night huffing dry-cleaning fluid. Dawn
            dirties to world. Calls his P.O. from the vaulted
            sanctum above the recovery basement.

            Outside, smoking a number, a car, door open, stopped in the street.
            A body, prone, in front of it.
            No one around.
            Hero gets in, gets a new him.

Terror, fungible, in lingerie, gauche and unregenerate.
Help find his opinion. A four-letter word for it. Everyone's monster.
En masse, the crash and condolence of wings,
the singe and musculature. Made from Monad.

3rd line: Through a surveillance camera, overexposed,
            anorexic palm trees boulevard to a coil of whose. . .
            Boy: bad movie.
            Girl: bad f/x.
        White Boy: good story, though.
        White Girl: good boy.
            Boy: burn one thing, what?
            Girl: school.
        White Boy: your momma
        White Girl: the ocean.

Not a human friend but a residue of unconsciousness.
Not addiction but a shout of silk. An ambience.
Infinity's twin eyes.
They twine in front of the monitors, in a tangle of tubing.
Fire, fire, story, fire.

4th line: Wearing a sandwich board—BODY COUNT

$$105,007/\infty\text{—}$$

        outside the switchyard
                where the plotlines compound &
        part flowchart part orgy

                Explains to the looping, fly-sized camera
        that in S.E. Asia 3,000 years ago
        lived from whom we all descend
                        one man/ woman

        A child enters the frame and flips the final digit to 8 (infinity
        verticalized)

        Plot kisses the boy, who recoils.

Habeas Corpus

As if on wheels
.   the hotel coasts
cop-slow up Ocean Avenue, stops.

No cigarettes, no lip-balm, lungs, father, gender, culture.

A breeze, Grecian perhaps, yawns
slowly inside an awning, shawls

me in its, excess of sense, sex—
on whose sad canvas
a neon dolphin signals, flickeringly:
H o t e l
        D e l f i n , Vacancy.

The architecture, say, like the square
root of Miami less LA, a pastel poise
without apparent purpose. I zoom in.
The doors blaze open, coronal and

            Desk clerk
says well, I'm policed to meet you. His teeth scritch,
        Says   no but   we don't
I mean   Don't we   here Take
            one can   Haven't we   Every
        See   Time it's like yours   amethyst
            your wrists   your arrest   and demi-
semiquaver   dress   let's
            let's for one   once
so fragile where your wings   Lucifer's
                no   his sheriff's no   don't you think
        after the twentieth   after our tryst
        bomb   at the Holy Land
        Theme Park   sweetheart   what would
one   blister   so

I put his cigarette out with my eyes.
I walk to the fireplace, put my hand in the flames.
He sticks the fire extinguisher's nozzle down his throat. So there's hope.

Rave

Ravel of ravishments the raven-black
interstices   of the cat-walked
factory-guts.   Below which the revelers
their engines   *rêve*
overheating   the revelers orchidized
with chemical, chimerical crystals of x.

It is a scene, Act X.
               A small door
opens high in the mind: two girls
with daisy stickers on their nipples
slip into the mix, while
              phased lights agitate and valve
the crowd, as toward an epilepsy or cure.
The DJ puts the song into reverse, lets it out
then backs again. No one belongs to their bodies as to a paternalistic order
        anymore;
balloons of anaesthetic gas pass hand to hand and when
the mind returns it finds itself inside
another's numbed, Apollonian torso.

One of the ones one was wanders
all night in this way, *ill-assorted, contra-*
        dictory.
Looking for his legs. A whisper craven in the dregs.

—(*Excep*)t:

It is The Earth here too. Overburdened with product, with invention.
Restorative in its seasonal self-destructions, tectonic musics

Clang and Rattle, Bang, Shake, Rock and Roll

And although we have learned to live inside our bodies without irony   without
        completion
when from miles within the unearned earth   we could have loved you
high heaved over us   waves of breaking glass   a force catches
        fire
and which seems   in falling frames   to just hang there
        arresting you

General of the Casing Air

Rain is a mansion ruin fashions, as gravity's the
graffiti
falling scrawls us through and thorough. I crawl and trough with it.

In the Palace of False Surplus, the aphorists
fête themselves with sweetmeats and sour rose.
They do not rise, unrealized, or against.

Prices are falling. Failing is falling.

Surf-thick insolvencies overrun the upturned
plenum of the trumpet flowers—medium-rare mirage,
miraculous devastation.

(To wit: he feeds the wedding dress to the shredder.
To wit: mid-parable, perishables spoil in full view
of the need whose serenade they were or are).

Rain with its get-rich-quick, its letters writ in smudge and bludgeon,
its surfeit and seizure loosening the money-swollen hillside
whereon the multimillionaire's airy redoubt
(part Spanish mission, part space shuttle)
purchases less and less that's solid,
its heron-leg supports flame-flimsy and then
the whole over-elaborate grift-work
tumbled gorgeward

~

I knew a ruin of a girl, the rain reminds, named Rain,
who never wore shoes and whose tear ducts— rusted
shut with some precipitate of perpetual, grievous wonder—reddened ever.

Some years later, I hear, her boyfriend kidnaps her and ties her
to a dead pine at the place of their first seduction.

But she was already broken everywhere it mattered.
She was indefinite and plural as rain and when he
returned with an armload of firewood, gone.

~

Because it's easy to rebuild what never was
the rain conflates utopia and ruin.

~

It would make rich, moldering tropics of these topical
hills, inform each secret weeping-place in the irreparable
roof—

as on Channel Seven, toppled angels
issue, hissing, from the fallen transformer
and are, for once, the first end of a naïve return
through cleansing violence
to inorganic unconsciousness.

~

Reaction shot: Cosentino's Nursery, on Las Flores Rd., below
the kindergarten (*childgarden*) where I learned to alphabetize
the petals of flowers, my defoliate thoughts—

the baby bougainvillea, the potted imported orchids,
elephants ears and bonsai pines, as from a sundered ark
put to sea. The TV goes, and then the power—
only a game show of rain, rain's
homilizing dramas and comedies. I am seventeen

while all around rises a name for myself,
writ on water's written matter, its scrambled heights.

Below, on the hillside, eighty-year-old aspirin
bottles bob up through the loam.

Tar Pits

Here your unmarked –ings your plena runneth
unruined barrel/week
your thin, been scrim grossed on gloss
your tar-in-the-lungs tared stars stares
your rubbery, fresh parking lots

Enough, then, by now, to pave from
one *me* one *you*, either/or down any street.

To force the shapeful hates of un-earth into cages, losses, closets.
Runways. Best Sleep Ever. Pays-the-Rent [hearts] Sitting-Shiva.

Rely joy ram end. Rock tar rebel. Rate clerk rob

(X eat, edge, **end**, entry)

Where the spam affects queue, *gnikcab rorrim*
            perforated to exact all objects
from your System Into,

churn furniture from furnace:
golfball afloat in a jumbo soda, visual
flotsam, donuts, gloves, provenance

                    ~

Something he does on the side—like help, like
            wanting to help
people plead *help*; fetal means and meanders
spread into the unwed
surround of streets to doors we do dare open: dire wolves and day
laborers
countersunk into divinity's last good drunk: statutes and statuettes
proud
around a rage every attempt to bail
weights
with waiting.

"He that toucheth tar, cannot but be defiled thereby."
Read: to beat the tar out of: tar-acne, -lamp, -paper, -baby.
". . .butter for fat sheepe. . ." ". . .as a boy does a wasp's nest. . . "

Two movements: x made axe and cast bell,
wrecking ball and beachcomber.

"Scattered over great tracts of wild country, California
smells of it, and very pleasantly."

~

We trade two stereos for a five-pack of *history iceberg*
and another five of *drop zone* and sit down
various in sodium light—spoon, flame, belt, spike,
accoutrements of obit ibid rep, heart like a floor safe.

And the bird's-eye-sized zero-dimensional endstop of product.
Tie off, punch the clock, sinks the sky, as such.

~

In the shakeout, comes pesticide, comes polyester.
Chewing gum, detergent, mustard gas precursor.
Heart valves, condoms, contact lenses, synthetic thought.

Crawls from chiaroscuro, progress' emblem or figure
the rising ground, in absolute difference, monsters.
Back in the refusing sludge, what threat—
not-me and not-me, mastodon the mascot
of a massed difference we cannot reckon into
the new total, teeth marks in the spine and fibula.

Weasels, crested eagles,
figures the "insomnia of thought" uproots,
lets as black flames leap from the abyss, Pleistocene
bestiary, a totem pole of eaten eating, class struggle
the combustions of which soufflé our grid, dirge, girders.

I am, without concept. Capital's tarbaby
larded up with lugnuts and languish, zits, pistols.
I, the cheapest real estate. I, incompletion, unincorporated
infinity, -ist. Stuck the more I struggle to moralize
my way a harrow from halo.

Now we are both one thing aggression
glues together, which exercise power dreams.
Find me here, in my sarcophagus of preservatives,
with my record of airborne toxins, poisoned water, sick earth—
disease which is its own cure, machine which works by breaking down

The Subject who, Must, needs say, of Objects

                                        (bottlecap, jewelcase, business-card)
a viscous field weighing down what's waiting there
to be measured against another late arrival

Scared, or am, combustions which soufflé the grid
awash with desiderated vehicles

Every ten years for an epoch,   a teratorn or ground
sloth, a mastodon   or western horse
not yet hunted to extinction   not yet
fallen through an overlay of   quilted leaves
we might describe, fallen through the failure of metaphor
to say to capital, or genetics

And then the big sabertoothed cats arrive   the Pleistocene bestiary piling up
orgiastic, eating each other, mired the more they struggle
against the non-moral of the non-story

about the appreciation of real estate, life-soaked
and heart-soaked and animal, the crude, vivacious ooze

bubbled up to pave the highways and power the televisions—
by way
of, wave on wave—

Elegy on Preemption Rd.

Desert, *which presupposes loss*. Which underwrites desire / sent to bed
without dessert. Deserters from the war on where

camped in trailers. A plagiary in the sense processors:

less place than procedure / than camouflage
slammed into category. You bet.

Just try scribbling a thousandth in that cloud.
Is this what being right feels like, like
liking less and less you can't demolish at a glance

from which a lesser man of me might run?

A red dirt road which ends in the dry wrath the gestural
Joshua trees
vanishing into hearty symbolic orders?
Boulders
the shakedown horizons won't allow to shoal like shade spoils
sun uncouples from its steamroll?

~

This system is dangerously low on resources
Mailer-Daemon: Host Unknown

~

First pitch: plot snapping on its chain
as a Star might, under a 10x lens,
runs his role down to pure rule, Harley gleam
and harlequin distilling speed from a mixture of injured
air and pop psychology.

Nothing rusts, nothing rots or rats out what's
soured to a doppler of stills.
In the mirror, mom is mom, irreversible.
In the wrong end of the camera, wow.

~

To the west, a replica movie set of a ghost town
abandoned and therefore become, finally,
what it had ciphered and siphoned,

as a personage might eventually
tell itself to fate.

East: Marines awash in a hardening mirage
they call Iran or Syria.
South: exurbs, money swamps and verdant
sweeps the eye fertilizes.
North: north
Here: her cirrhosis, her seizure

~

If wonder is another's mirror-mourning.
If beauty was the death of mother,
beauty the Motherdeath Of.

~

All that's false gets outsourced here for processing,
archived or deleted or cordoned off in falls of sky
that what's called true might gets its parade
in red, white and blue,
the west won and war turned warm.

The rest of us test positive, miraculous mirage.

Every Star Will Be in its Place

Hot as shock treatment, a cure in the care of Mojave wind
Rewinds the trains in Union Station
Back to a hexed clock: Poincaré's

Paris of simultaneity which gallows you
Among the turbid stars of never before.

By the riverine shimmer of the Mission walls
Two palominos, browsing by torchlight, bronze,
And their tails swat, one last time,

At the foregone colonies of stars
Replaced by glass-sconced gaslights
On a parabolic ceiling. Smallpox

Scars of 'burbs, scare stares, paid back in the burning groins
In the rough, untranslated rock of news perhaps
From Death Valley: no gas, no water, nowhere to elapse.

~

It's 1940 again. It's Theodor Adorno again
Thrown from the unmoving train into the speeding
Carousel of the basin, under a crush of tuberculars

And aspirations, slow cancers, bad teeth.
Terza rima! an infernal machine
Twirls its baton outside Kaiser Steel.

And the winner is. . . . If a train is the dream
Of a failing horse, a rocket
the hanged man's last fuck, paid by the page,

Each frame a corneal layer peeled
From the stunned eyes of sunbathers.
The feel of this hedonizes with the vested, bestial interests.

Every train station's a massacre—winds
Piling up deep into the heart rate,
Into the infiltration of figural painting into a world

Without a scissors, without world.

~

Behind the theaters, joy thrown from the parboiled minds
Piped out to reinforce
Someone else's misfortune. No homes, only houses.

City of abbreviations—each condensed to a catch-phrase.
No protest in Protestantism, no test in testicles—
One life no less or more than another

And therefore worthless, filed under "closed."
A uniform solitude draws the dollar-shaped trolley tracks
Through the orange smell of oblivion.

One likes to lick the blood from a map.
One likes to think of himself as a pill on the tongue of God.
These powers, these strong waters!

That I-am gaze beaten back by red perfumes!

~

The naive thought of a return to naiveté
Not naive enough to cure us of this radiocast
Ratiocination, split odds.

Pictures without images or images without pictures,
Form so deeply abstracted that it's formless,
Chains us to the comic

Strip of statistical averages, mannikins in a streetcar.

And now not now but here we are, the out-of-tune Wagnerian
Reduction ocean
Banging its head against the jetty, the jettisoning point
Where the human consigns herself to a dim, defunct idea.

Dear me, dear me, we might have known to miss you.

Documents

1. [Delta of day laborers in the shape of Mesoamerica outside Fred Jordan's Skid Row Mission. Christmas, 1991.]
CITIBANK / Yeah, that's right. Get yours.

2. Socialism or Barbie!

3. I'll lend our eyes so you can see.
(*A siren like a risen sneer, like rain backwards; the backstory: just words*)
REAL TOTAL KAOS
Welcome to Mexico, white boy!

4. National Sick Day

5. *A Movie*—
A screen across the intersection: *after you.*
Three doors cut into the ocean water.
The middle one open, 888 Wilshire, tilting in the frame.
Then water, then ice, then desert.
Chinatown and Bunker Hill and the gulch of the Harbor Freeway
folded into a meadow, a landfill.
Through one door, a Gabrieleño hanging from a post.
Through another, a television filled with hands.
Through the third, lawn.

6. ¡Y!

7. Paperdolls cut from blow-ups of green cards barricade the onramps.
Traffic computers hacked at 9:07.
Every light in the westside red and stays so for five minutes,
horns chain, harmonic resonance, some flag, some gulf.

8. Billboard [Two sixty-year-old men fucking] And on the seventh day. . .

9. Target. Camouflage for Boredom.

10. Under the parking lot, the beach.
Under the beach, the parking lot.

11. Tape hiss of authenticity.

12. Billboard [A file of handcuffed, tagged men, mostly Black or Latino, led through a tasteful Scandinavian modern living room, carpet of snow, decorous shatters of glass]

13. No objects without rejects. Champion Market. Peace Market. Invest in your community. Police brutality is no surprise.

14. All gangs must soon younite. Armageddon culture revolution.

15.Unstoppable Painters—All Out Kaos
Leaving All Krushed—Masters in Art
One Evil Style—
On the Run—Public Nuisance—
Dow Zero Party.

16.Mist. Ozzie. SK8. Chubs. Perk. Lost. Dripster. Dream Room.
Bloods and Crips unite in peace. Do it for the children.

17.[Charred Laundromat] Look what you created. Tra la la.

Day Job

From Premonition Point, at century, sexed lights
darken which buildings were war, are.

Lawsquare and finish, blossom knots.

You can tell by following the ones bigger than at-once
(bloodstone, healstone, tooth) to the sorrying-block.

Oh, you've been noticing again, for real
like a third nature, like some kind of galactic
bone structure, a fingerprint on the princely marblefloss.

And the rickety databases, like kelp beds,
sway and yawn, offset by the roving coastline
you keep moving against, sunspikes
through the partially demolished
Ambassador Hotel. True and false.

~

My big white car a small black scar for sure
for every non-future peek-a-booing through the orphan mists.
I climb into the Hazmat suit with her.
Made a civilization, watched the ants
irradiate the pages of *Why I Am Not a Christian.*
Steak dinner. All-you-can-eat-crow. Mirrors
that walk, that festoon the topiary
heavens with public privacies, exo-affect.

~

Me too, you. My if-feeling and my or-feeling
labor in a synecdoche of shade, so a theorem results,
that bacterial time and intensive time in the coiffure of red now
might require measures too mean to intend.
I'm being rational, though, which doesn't really make sense.
We put on our compu-flesh and wait for
instructions from our remote correspondent:
homo negativa, eros degree zero auto-immune removal trees.

~

Nerd modernism. Wingless panoramas. Light, of course, and the wineglass
on the plate the only clock. A tissue of collided gazes from which a room
emerges, floor and far wall skewed so as to provide a maximal view.

~

Meanwhile, in the historical, methane
filling the pantry where Sirhan Sirhan
whispers something to his gun. An anti-Sinatra moment.
You too, you too.
Hello, Ike. Hello, Dick. Hello, Ron.

Run.

House: body with its insides adjusted.
Apartment building: birth collage.
Office tower: a squad of artists hiding the blood in micro-vials.
Street: without concept: air.

Alarum and Mural

(. . . with hyper-reflective foil and tonnages fungible as love;
            two turntables, one mike: switchboard and quilt—O!
blaze an intercontinental canal
inside the baroque, disposable life-paths
that ambit us with poor example!

Come out, come down, wherever you aren't!
Cry the post-emotive flexions
from plinths of meringue and stingy rewind

No more rigmarole casserole we'll ring
the shriveled scrota of the law, being liquid
has its mixed divisions, don't think

A rose is a ruse is a route eros
short-circuits but we're shoutin' down
a big fuck no, we're not allowed to stabilize
that headgear for longer than a beer commercial

Has it really gotten to the point where you can't slice the monuments from
the moment without
taking off your fingerprints too?

Going about my business in a solution
of obsessive-compulsive if-then loops
beauty subtracts, whipsnap smashmouth,
skirting the CPU and the House of Cool,
a scheme occurs to me to travel
both ways at once down Ohio Avenue

Brusque projections over the mundanities and onramps—
new skies, Psych! Welcome to who
was it that played you in the essentially imageless version
checking your lipstick in the reflections in your watch

            free)(way
Origin and destination unbound in a bright
scatter of tail-lights—if free, then free *from* not *to* morph
or form aught, not license

nor insurance against arrival of the dull
for real, for sale, unfailingly lit
by combustible distributions

For public space, for center amidst
the fortress and clash of disordered main, this will have to do,
this shared isolation—screens, windshields
in phase with a frequency the songs close around the throat,
mute mouth moving behind glass alas all eyes
vectored to a stale vanish the smog cures

You cannot drive the same freeway twice
You cannot live here stable as an I
But neither can you become the music of these
swerves and drifts one errancy
might agglutinate, gigavariable complex
we have no math for yet,

lit by a field the discovery of which
might mean a Northwest passage
cut right through every home, car, tower
fear monumentalizes

But also a diagram of disenfranchisement,
a place you cannot lie down or stand up in,
line of flight the wake of which erupts

~

April 30th, 1992: preteens in the embankment ivy
lobbing bottles into traffic, watermelons, hormonal badges, textbooks,
a gamelan of things the hinges of which game and bull's-eye

Mid-arc: the fires catch in the: bottles
key the sickened, high-tempt
testures of solace milked from miked isolation, no I,
kitty-corner from the piss-smell and ketamine phone booth

All politics is property damage. All property a rubber bullet rubbed in dope.
This is the equation their graffiti writes—
prosody of names homes such that either
joy or despair in hot pursuit. Hotsuit.

At the aerospace complex, the rocket engines, firing bellyup, suck
the neighborhoods into maw
worthless and hence invaluable.

Police sprout in the sites of permanent scaffolding.
Video-camera technology cheap enough to disturb
the subject-object sluice

~

"I'm kind of tired of being me, I guess," Wind said

~

Walking in Los Angeles is like dancing in wet cement.
The distances cheat. You make the city up.
Channels of light and dark symposium on squirm and offer
something glorious about to happen, a kind of art or tar
whose hardening a steady, moderate movement postpones.
Joyous rifts and perpendicularities rupture.
Umbrage of palms, psalm, wet mural of lips.
Follow the fuzziness, cyclone fencing, the riptip
affect buzzsawed police Interceptor
from which the post-punk mariachis rainbow,
from which the black and white and man and woman
make keys of a piano, pinot, no.
A kabbalah of consanguinity, all the eclectic do-it-yourself architecture with hands.
You could land a plane in her heart.

Acknowledgments

Versions of these poems appeared in *Absent*, *Xantippe*, *Aiden Starr*, and in *The Iowa Anthology of New American Poetries*: thanks to the editors of these publications. To the friends who read and commented on versions of this book, especially Joshua Corey, Melanie Boyd, Gina Franco, Chris Nealon, Geoffrey G. O'Brien, Karl Parker, David Weiss and the late, much missed Deborah Tall: my abiding gratitude. To Joshua Clover, for his friendship and faith in this project: innumerable thanks. To Charles Legere, for his design acumen, thank you. Finally, to those whose works and lives I describe or quote herein (friends, enemies, strangers, family): this book is yours too.